The Story I'll Tell

Natalie M. Ashby

authorHOUSE®

AuthorHouse™
1663 Liberty Drive
Bloomington, IN 47403
www.authorhouse.com
Phone: 833-262-8899

Published by AuthorHouse 09/01/2021

ISBN: 978-1-6655-3562-5 (sc)
ISBN: 978-1-6655-3560-1 (hc)
ISBN: 978-1-6655-3561-8 (e)

Library of Congress Control Number: 2021917230

Print information available on the last page.

Any people depicted in stock imagery provided by Getty Images are models, and such images are being used for illustrative purposes only. Certain stock imagery © Getty Images.

This book is printed on acid-free paper.

CONTENTS

DEDICATION

In loving memory of my husband who is
missed greatly and loved forever ~

to my children, Anna and Dustin, Josh and Bekah, Sarai and Ashby
and Aaron and Lauren who provide strength, humor, life and love ~

to my grandchildren who are the joy and light of my life ~

to my dear friends who have been supportive,
encouraging and my source of laughter ~

and to my heavenly Father who has kept me and
strengthened me during this journey ~

FOREWORD

Our Christian literature and bookshelves are filled with biographies and autobiographies of men and women of God who shares stories of triumph, tragedy and journeys that are touched by the empowering grace of God. Most of these are written from the "first chair" position, and you rarely find one that shares the journey of a wife, widow or ministry partner, particularly after the significant ministry partner has graduated to their reward in heaven. Even fewer are those who combine the story of their journey with powerful devotional truths that call us to the identity that God has created us to live in that is not attached to ministry or family roles or circumstances.

This beautiful story told by Natalie Ashby is unique in the revelation and process of entering into the season of life where she shares how to live out the fullness of the dream of God for your life, regardless of all the challenges that are presented to women in our culture and church to stay locked into identities that are more about roles and function rather than in the glory of one who is created by God for purpose and glory, and to live in the power of His love for all eternity. She writes from a place of authority, as a pastor's wife, a pastor in her own right, ministry school director and powerful woman of God. Your heart will be strengthened and your joy expanded as you take in the stories that this "woman of wonder" tells in these pages. As you walk through the 21 days of encouragement, God's Word and

Spirit will speak and bring strength for this season of your life. Drink it in, all this glorious telling and declaring of God's faithfulness.

Dr. Mike Hutchings, Director
Global Awakening School of Ministry, Mechanicsburg, PA
gssmusa.com
President, God Heals PTSD Foundation
GodHealsptsd.com

"It's hard to imagine making a vow to love and honor 'til death parts you and then it does. Devotion never looked so bittersweet. It seems odd to celebrate an anniversary of 37 years when he's not here. Their wedding album was destroyed in a fire but the photos are still clear in my mind. I used to stare at her beautiful dress and his signature serious expression lit by candlelight in my grandfather's church. Their hands, their rings, their faces young and unaware. Mr. and Mrs. James Ashby walked down an aisle that stretched out for 35 years with every step of faith. Ask her about it sometime. She's got a lot of wisdom and anecdotes to share. Happy Anniversary."

Anna Ashby Ayers

INTRODUCTION

He told me the 'R' in James R. Ashby stood for
Romeo. I fell for it head over heels.
James and I married in June of 1983 after six months of dating
and serving together in ministry for almost two years.
We had three children, Anna, Josh and Sarai
by 1989...the joy of our lives.
We entered full-time ministry in 1993; I continued working
so we had consistent income and insurance for our family.
Our fourth child, Aaron, was born in 1995...more joy
and the one all of my older kids call "the favorite".
James was ordained as a Bishop in the
Church of God in the early 1990s.
We pastored three different churches between 1993
and 2017; although it was necessary for me to keep
working outside the home, moving to accommodate
a new pastorate was always considered primary.
James worked a secular job in addition to his Senior Pastor position
all of our married lives. He took good care of his family.
He served on the Church of God Youth Board and the Evangelism
Board multiple times during his ministry, as well as serving as
Head of the Usher Committee during state conventions and
Risk Management Team member for national conventions.

We began new challenges outside of pastoral ministry.
James was treated for prostate cancer in 2007. We were shocked at the
diagnosis but thankful there were no disruptions in ministry or family
responsibilities during his relatively quick treatment and recovery.
That same year our young daughter had twin girls
with significant physical needs. She and her daughters
lived with us until she married in 2016.
In 2009, we had a house fire in the church parsonage and lost
all of our possessions. I didn't really have anything especially
precious to me but all our photos. I had so many photo albums
and decorated almost exclusively with family pictures and school
portraits of my children. All of those were gone. We nearly lost
our sons. Our young son received only very minor injuries.
My husband developed a brain tumor in September 2012.
This started a whole new trajectory in our lives.
I actually completed my MBA sitting in a
hospital room at my husband's bedside.
James was diagnosed with CNS lymphoma of the brain in May 2013.
He received intense chemotherapy treatments at Duke
University Hospital from June 2013 through May 2014.
He received radiation treatments in June
2014 thus defeating the cancer.
The devastating effects of the chemotherapy and radiation increased
over time until he was no longer able to pastor the church where
we had served for almost 18 years. Somewhere in this time, I began
taking over the responsibilities of the church, the leadership team,
the home and the family. I began making every single decision.
This was not a position I wanted but it seemed to be the only
way to allow him to pursue his calling in such a poor physical
state. I made these decisions with humility, trying to determine

what he would have done without causing him added stress or further anxiety. During this time, at the request of my husband, I received my minister's license through our denomination.
We moved out of the church parsonage into our own townhouse in another city in October 2016. He stayed in the parsonage alone on the night we moved. He did not want to leave.
We stopped pastoral ministry in February 2017. He was not happy about this decision. His heart wanted to continue.
His mind and body would not cooperate with his heart.
We began attending another church in another city in February 2017. He was no longer known as the Bishop. He became reserved, quiet and disengaged. He didn't know where he belonged. It was so hard to watch this transformation.
In spite of everything, he continued to inspire others and prayed for so many.
James went to Heaven on Palm Sunday, April 14, 2019.
It was just like him to go on a day of great celebration!

CHAPTER 1

Don't Call Me That

Widow.

I hate the word.

It screams helplessness, brokenness and loneliness. It depicts a loss of identity along with grief and pain.

I never understood women who seemed they could not get along independently. I always felt like I was independent. I had four children. Three of them I handled alone most of the time as my husband worked in the shipyard seven days a week 12-, 14-, 16-hour days. I would feed the children, dress them, pack their lunches, pack the diaper bag, pack book bags, go to the school, go to the babysitter's, go to work, go to the grocery store, cook, clean, do laundry, bathe the children, put them to bed and then do it all over again. Somewhere in there, I would play music and sing at church; I would teach Sunday School and Wednesday night Youth Bible Class. Later, when the kids were in high school and college, I worked and traveled alone for several years in the corporate world. I was independent, or so I thought.

I married when I was 19 and he was 27. He was older and seemed so much wiser about the world. I was sheltered...very sheltered. I was raised in a very conservative Pentecostal pastor's home. There were so many things that were not discussed in our home. I relied on my husband

1

to teach me about life, the world, marriage and so many other things. This was the beginning of the development of my identity as the wife.

Before we had our third child in the fifth year of our marriage, my husband and I began our preparation for pastoral ministry. Within a few years, we were pastoring a church. My husband was raised in an even more conservative Pentecostal pastor's home. In his childhood home, the church came first. His father was always on call. The members took priority. This was the responsibility. My husband pastored in a similar way yet still seemed to find time for family. He had a compassionate heart and took his role seriously.

For so many, the identity of pastor, husband and father can roll over into one another. The stress of not only raising a family but also carrying the burdens of parishioners can be overwhelming. It is sometimes easier to stay in pastor mode than it is to transition back to husband and father. I remember more than once saying "please do not be my pastor, I need my husband". It was a cry for intimacy and relationship, not a defiance against his role. He had a knack for coaching people to be better and encouraging them to rise above. He was a strong tower for those who felt weak and unable to stand on their own. He was a former football player with broad shoulders, a confident stance, and could strike up a conversation with anyone. I was much more reserved. I was quiet, withdrawn, the one who was terribly uncomfortable with flattery and pleasantries. I could tell when he was in "coach" or "preacher" mode. He had the charisma of a motivational speaker that made you feel like you could tackle every demon with a water gun by the time he was done talking to you. When it came time for him to talk to me or to deal with a family issue, we didn't want to be coached much of the time. We wanted to be heard and understood. It was not always clear where the line was drawn. Being the pastor's wife required an understanding that he was always the pastor....and I was always the pastor's wife.

It was a revelation to me that after my husband died, I did not know who I was. I did not realize it, but for so long I had been an extension of my husband. I married early, never living alone, always doing what pleased my father, always considering the desires of my mother, always staying within the church guidelines. I never had to determine what my own identity looked like, what my personal preferences were, how I wanted to live. I went from pleasing my parents to pleasing my husband without ever learning what was actually important to me. This is not a complaint, it is a reality.

Once I was married, it became normal to do what was necessary to survive. The first child set the focus for me for years to come. It was more about raising them to successful adulthood. I believe we did that well. I am incredibly proud of each one of our children. Their gifts, talents and callings along with their personalities, humor and generosity are incredible. I have thought many times, if I did nothing else, I raised great human beings!

The first few months after my husband died, I was again in survival mode. I knew I had to sell our townhouse for financial reasons. Because of that and the fact that three of the four children lived out of state, I had to sort through all my husband's things right away. I let the children take whatever they wanted, made bears out of Papa's shirts for the grandchildren and kept things that were dear to me. My focus went into selling the house, packing and putting belongings in storage. I stayed with each of my daughters for a period of time. This was a great distraction for me as I had grandchildren to play with, kids to talk to and no real responsibilities other than work.

About four months into widowhood, I found a little apartment near the church I attend. It was just big enough for a couch, a recliner, a desk, a bed, a dresser and a nightstand. It was all I needed as I now lived alone.

Alone.

What a singular word … alone. I could have a gray couch if I wanted it. I could have a red chair if I wanted it. No one else was there to consider their likes, opinions, decisions. What did I want? Was I sure I wanted that? Was it okay to want that? I had never made decisions based solely on what I wanted. All of a sudden, it was overwhelming. It took me MONTHS to decide on a living room rug … a RUG!

You have to understand that even when I thought I wanted something before, I would end up making decisions based on someone else's thoughts, feelings and likes. When I bought my first car at the age of 46, I bought the vehicle I was told was a better car, a smarter buy and more comfortable fit. I didn't even TEST DRIVE the car I actually liked and wanted to consider buying.

Growing up and later raising my family in a church parsonage did not allow for much creativity. The walls had to be off white. The carpet could not be replaced. The appliances were the same that they always were. I was finally able to pick paint colors for the walls of the parsonage that was replaced when we had a house fire losing nearly everything. Even then I was so concerned about what everyone else thought.

Once I was in my little apartment, it was very overwhelming to go grocery shopping or go out to eat. I had always based my shopping and restaurant choices based on someone else's needs or wants. There were times I just wouldn't go shopping or out to eat simply because the decision was too hard to make. Pasta? Steak? Fish? Burger? Skipping dinner was better than the mental torment I was putting myself through.

I have heard people say, "Now you can do whatever you want". That sounds nice but it really screams, "You're alone!" How do you help others understand that it is not the freedom of choice that makes you happy but having someone to share these choices is what is important?

I used to be proud of my independence. Now that it is a status and not a choice, I'm not so crazy about the idea. I found out that I really was not that independent. I was simply able to function when I was alone. I was able to travel, work, shop, eat out and work out by myself, but I was always able to come home to someone who loved and needed me.

What is my purpose when no one needs me at home? How do I determine my self-worth when no one acknowledges me? It is very natural for a woman to be a nurturer, a caregiver and one who meets the needs of others. But when the children are grown and the spouse is gone, there is no one to nurture and no one to care for.

This all began the search for my identity.

CHAPTER 2

Who Am I?

It's funny how you think you know all about yourself until everything you have always known is pulled out from under you. Motherhood did not go away; however, the way I mother is now different. I don't have little ones around my ankles requiring every moment of attention. I don't have school age children who require rides to school or ball games or needing school clothes or supplies. I don't have teens or college students in my home anymore. Motherhood now has me asking my adult children for their advice; staying in touch with them because I need them in my life; going to visit them instead of insisting they come see me; and spending as much time as possible with my grandchildren.

For some people who suffer loss, the identities are lost all at once. Loving wife one moment, then grieving widow the next. It didn't happen to me that way.

My wife status changed a while back. It was so subtle. We had conquered the prostate cancer without much ado. A few doctor visits, an outpatient procedure, some rest, and James was good to go. The brain tumor was such an invasion into our lives. He never wanted to go to the doctor. He was in denial that anything was ever wrong. We went to church on Sunday. Our friend and church leader said he looked like he had had a stroke. I knew it wasn't a stroke. I've worked in healthcare for a while. I knew the symptoms. He "preached" that day from a sitting position. It was not really a message but some exhortation as he could not make or follow any notes. Right after church, I drove him to the emergency room. This is where we learned of the tumor in the brain. I looked at the doctor, and fresh, hot tears rolled down my face. I had no words to say. I simply sat there. I don't even remember what James had to say. I'm sure he was just in shock. I went outside to call our children. No one wants to call their children with this kind of news. We always want to be the strong ones. We always want to be the ones with the right answers. I called our son, Josh, first. He wasn't really following closely to the Lord at the time. But his words to me were, "Mom, we have always lived by faith. Don't worry." I then called our daughters, Anna and Sarai. They were encouraging, trying to be strong for me, but I know they were scared and deeply concerned. This was a hard hit. I called our son, Aaron. He was just starting his senior year of high school. He was working out at the baseball gym when I called. He broke down. I broke down…again. He told me later that his coach hugged him and prayed with him. We didn't know then that James would miss his graduation. James would miss his wedding.

I didn't realize the moment when I moved from wife to caregiver; it was like driving a car over an ice-covered road – this illness had a mind of its own and I was just trying to make sure we didn't crash. At some point, I was needed to provide quality care and ensure safety, medication management, provider networking and transportation. It probably does not happen like this to everyone. When you are caring for someone whose efforts are concentrated on staying alive, battling treatments, going to numerous doctor visits and trying to be comfortable each day, the focus changes from serving one another, being the partner your spouse desires, engaging in family affairs and planning for the future to mere survival.

My pastor's wife status changed when the decision was made to resign from pastoral ministry. There was no more teaching, preaching, leading worship, making leadership decisions, coordinating the leadership team, moderating services and tending to the needs of the congregation. There was also no longer a community of people that I was comfortable with. I had a few friends but not anyone so close that they would stay engaged. It was like being let go once their pastor was not there. I recognize how difficult it must have been on the parishioners to have their pastor leave due to health issues when they had prayed for him for so long. It must have felt like abandonment to them. To me, it just felt like loneliness.

Not a wife, not a doting mother, not a pastor's wife, not a caregiver... who was I? What do I do now? Yes, I had a job, but it was not my life. Yes, I went to church, but it was not the same by myself. I felt lost, confused, scared, anxious, insecure, lonely... I blamed myself for things that were not my fault. I questioned many things about myself, heaping on self-condemnation and humiliation.

Not long after moving out of pastoral ministry and moving into a new church environment, James and I attended a class that taught about blessings, identity and destiny. During one of the ministry moments, the leader of our group was praying and ministering to me. I did not know her prior to that weekend. I know she has a good heart, hears from God and seeks to impart truth. During her ministry time, she told me I had pride. I prayed about the pride. I certainly do not want to be prideful. However, I am not totally convinced it was pride. I am more inclined to believe it was more of convincing myself I was okay. I had to intentionally hold my head up, concentrate on not breaking down at any moment and continue to move in a productive way. I cannot help but think how many times people are mislabeled, misunderstood or misinterpreted simply because others do not take the time to understand where an individual may be in their walk, the way they are processing life or struggling with grief or pain.

I decided to do individual coaching to help me transition in a healthy way. When I started doing sessions with the Minister's Coach to learn who I was, I could not even answer simple questions. My coach would ask me questions about my core desires, and I could not answer them. I had lived a life of reaction and response to others for so long, I was missing. It took several weeks to get to the core of who I am as an individual.

I have learned that I have core desires. I want to be thought of as good. I never want to give the impression that I am not good enough, that I have failed, that I am not worthy, or that I am not perfect. I have learned that when I do fail, it can take me some time to recover. I overanalyze because I want to be sure my motives and my actions are pure. I have learned that my sins, failures and imperfections are covered by the blood of Jesus. I know that I am created in the image of God. I know that God sees the righteousness of His Son in me and not my imperfections. I know how to detox my thoughts, replacing accusing, defaming, negative thoughts with the truth of the Word of God. I have learned that this must be done routinely; it is not a one-time only process. I have learned that God can use me in my imperfect state. He can use me in my failures, insecurity, confusion, anxiety or fear.

During the time we were dealing with my husband's decline in health, I would struggle with his attitude, my attitude, his depression, my guilt, our lack of communication, my weakness, our pain. I was serving on the Altar Ministry Team one Sunday. I was battling in a very real way. My emotions were a wreck. I felt worthless. I felt incapable of praying for anyone. I was not going to go up to be on the prayer team, but I felt the Holy Spirit nudge me to go on and minister. A lady came directly to me for prayer. When I asked her what she wanted prayer for, it was like I was listening to myself. She said almost verbatim the very things I was battling. It was like God was saying, "I see you; I know where you are; I know what you are feeling; I care about you". I prayed for her. God touched her. God touched me. I could feel an overflow of God's love. I could feel His strength helping me to stand. I felt my joy being restored. I could tell that God was doing the same for the lady I prayed for. We both received breakthrough that day.

I have learned that God can minister to me as I minister to someone else. I serve on a personal ministry team where we spend about four hours with an individual to help them receive inner healing from previous and present hurt. God has shown me so much of myself as I sit through these sessions, listening to women's stories, hearing how they have reacted to life's circumstances, seeing how they have built up walls to protect themselves. I can relate to so many of these women. I learned long ago how to build an emotional wall of protection. Being mocked when I was young because of the way we lived, being rejected as a pastor's wife, dealing with those who took advantage of my children and grieving the loss of my father and then my husband, I knew how to hide, how to recoil, how to walk tough like I didn't care. As I walk ladies through their healing of the soul, God reaches in and heals another layer of my own heart. Sometimes He transforms the lack of love I have for myself, and pours in the healing oil of everlasting love. Sometimes He helps me to recognize that one little thing I need to forgive and gives me grace to do so. Other times He brings peace into a situation over which I feel I have no control. Then there are times that He confirms His calling and destiny in me.

My family was raised with a great sense of humor, very dry, very sarcastic and sometimes even intellectual. You really had to have a quick wit to stay in the game. My dad and brothers were relentless. The more they attacked you with words (fun and feisty, not mean and ugly), the more you felt their love. I remember my daughter, Sarai, was young, her brother, Josh, would get her going. She asked me, "Mom, I need some comebacks." I had to let her know that they had to come from the heart, one does not get them from someone else. She worked on her responses. She's pretty good now.

Up until about three years ago, when someone asked how I was doing, I would respond "lovely". If it was a particularly hard day, I would say "stinking lovely". I never described myself as lovely and meant it. It was usually said in a sarcastic or cynical way. My kids, their spouses and I went to a Christian conference. One of the prophetic words I received was that God saw me as lovely and there was no flaw in me. I then found a piece of artwork at the conference showing beautiful flowers in my favorite color and the word LOVELY written on the page. Other words of affirmation (masterpiece, daughter of the King, pure, captivating, princess, beloved, etc.) were also written there, but LOVELY was written bolder and more distinctly. This piece of artwork hangs in my home where I can see it all the time. The scripture at the bottom says, "You are altogether lovely, there is no flaw in you" (Song of Solomon 4:7). Now when I say "lovely" to describe myself, I mean it. If God said it, it must be true.

A dear friend of ours, John, loved to remark about my abilities to manage a family, a full-time job, ministry, caregiving and anything else I needed to do. My daughter and her twin girls who had significant physical challenges lived with us during the time of my husband's cancer and treatments. I helped her with the girls' care, doctor visits and therapy appointments. During my husband's cancer, treatment and challenges, I would drive him to Duke Cancer Center three hours from home. I would have my work computer and work from the waiting room, the doctor's office and hospital room. I even finished my MBA while sitting in the hospital room. During the time of his treatments, my work required that I travel from one to three times each month. I would schedule my travel in between his treatments. When his hospital visits would go into the weekend, I would drive home the three hours on Saturday night or Sunday morning, lead worship and preach, then turn around and go back to the hospital. Every time John would see me, he would call me Wonder Woman. The term Wonder Woman has stuck over the years.

A couple of months after my husband went to be with Jesus, I was in Texas with my daughter. I was having a particularly difficult day. I was very emotional. I was frustrated with myself for not being able to keep it together. Trying to make light of the situation, I told my daughter that I was losing my Wonder Woman status. She looked at me, then walked to her kitchen, pulled a Wonder Woman cup out of her cabinet, brought it to the table where I was working, poured my Chick-Fil-A tea into the cup and said, "Here, you're still Wonder Woman! It's normal to cry and you should. Feel free to cry here, so you don't do it the wrong places, like in the middle of a meeting or something." I was so inspired by her response that I went out and bought myself a Wonder Woman cup and drink from it regularly.

Months later, I noticed that my Wonder Woman cup had a crack in the plastic. It wasn't really broken, but a little water was creeping in between the layers. So I bought a new Wonder Woman cup. I was looking at these cups and realized that although it is the same character, person, individual … it is a different version of who she is.

This is me.

I am still who I was… I am now just a different version of who I was.

I'm not lost.

I'm not forgotten.

I'm not forsaken.

I'm not less.

I'm a different version.

I am still Wonder Woman!

I am still effective!

I am still called!

I am still God's daughter!

I am still loved!

I am still unique!

I am ... still ~

Each day is an adventure to learn more of who I am. I am no longer just who I was told I was. In fact, I will always be in ministry in some facet. It may not look like what it used to but then I am not who I used to be. I'm no longer an extension of the great Bishop James Ashby. I am now just Natalie Ashby.

Just a daughter.

Just called.

Just royalty.

Just an heir.

Just a beautiful, lovely, worthy, beloved Wonder Woman of God.

CHAPTER 3

L is for Love ... or is it Loneliness?

This is a tough one.

After being married for a long time, then losing your spouse either through death or divorce, it is difficult being alone. Loneliness is difficult when you had a great marriage, an intimate relationship and a wonderful life. But even if your marriage was not ideal, even if your relationship was not perfect, even if your life was not always good, it is still hard to be alone.

As you begin to come out of the overwhelming grief into a different rhythm of life showered in grief, other emotions begin to emerge. There does come a time when you lift your head and see that there really are others out there to talk to, fellowship with and enjoy another's company. But then comes the question...How do you know when you want to be with someone if you are moving toward love or if you are just lonely?

I am the first one to say...I don't know the answer to this one. I have not crossed this threshold. Oh, I have pondered this for sure. In that pondering, I have learned some things.

Everyone who has suffered loss through death or divorce is still in pain. One little thing, a song, a phrase, a sound, a picture, a place, a word....any of these things can bring back a rush of memories. Things you thought were long forgotten. Things you thought were okay to move past. All of a sudden you're crying. You're in a zone. You're stuck. You're wondering, "What just happened"? It doesn't matter how long it's been. It still hits you sideways.

I have learned that this is normal... there is no judgment... it's going to happen.

I have also learned you cannot trust your emotions. They are up and down – happy and sad – hopeful and disappointed. Our emotions are erratic, unpredictable, inconsistent and sometimes blank. Our emotions are reflections of our experience, but they are not avenues for decisions or strategies for life. They cannot be trusted. They are reactive not proactive. They are responsive but not intentional. Still, our emotions are real and must be experienced. They are a gauge of where we are currently processing life, past, present and future.

Before moving toward love again, you must learn how to handle the loneliness. Love and loneliness cannot be confused. I had to come to an understanding that I can be fine just being by myself. I have learned (well, still learning) who I am. I am able to do my own thing, work my own schedule, plan my own activities, and all the rest. I CAN do things on my own. Fortunately for me, I was able to maneuver life by myself earlier in life. My husband and I were never attached to one another all day, every day, until the last five years of his life. Many couples have a very different dynamic, especially ministry couples who work in ministry together and are physically together 90% of the time. I strongly encourage any individual to have a community of family and friends. It is difficult to do this when your time is taken up with all the busyness. But we need community. God created us this way. We should build this community before we have to fully rely on it.

God was gracious enough to set me up with a wonderful group of friends a couple of years before my husband died. I have people that not only check on me but they also understand the process of grief, the battle with guilt, the accusations in my mind, the erratic emotions, and even the struggle to act normal. These friends have allowed me to be transparent but they have not allowed me to wallow in self-pity. They let me be honest without allowing me to give in to despair. My oldest son, who once worked in landscaping, told me that when sunflowers cannot get to the sun, they face each other. When I cannot make it on my own, I gain the strength to move forward through my friends and family.

When healing needs to occur following any kind of trauma, we have to allow the process to take place. Several years ago, I was in that place of not being sure what we were going through. I did not have understanding for what we were enduring. I doubted myself. I was full of anxiety, unrest and wanting to please but knowing I had to do things that were not going to be pleasing. My son, Aaron, had gone with me to speak with a minister friend. I had to not only get advice but I needed wise counsel. I had to make some very difficult decisions. Aaron told me I had to 'trust the process'. When I started directing a school of ministry, the underlying theme was Trust the Process. I think I got the message. There is a process. I must trust it. I am still trusting the process. It seems like one part of the process is completed, and then the process continues. The process is shown by Paul here:

I admit that I haven't yet acquired the absolute fullness that I'm pursuing, but I run with passion into his abundance so that I may reach the purpose for which Christ Jesus laid hold of me to make me his own. I don't depend on my own strength to accomplish this; however I do have one compelling focus: I forget all of the past as I fasten my heart to the future instead. I run straight for the divine invitation of reaching the heavenly goal and gaining the victory-prize through the anointing of Jesus.
(Philippians 3:12-14 TPT)

It is much easier to back out of the healing, pretend there is no pain, move on and jump into another relationship without having healed from the last. But this generates more pain, deeper wounds, unexplained responses, erratic behavior and even bitterness. God wants to heal our pain. He wants to remove the arrows that are still in our hearts. He wants to restore our souls. He wants to bind our wounds. But there is a process. The wounds of the heart are almost never healed in a moment, an hour, a day, a week or a month. These emotional healings take time.

When you are ready to move into a new relationship, do not expect that you will no longer have feelings for the one you lost. Those feelings will never go away. For someone to have touched your life so deeply, you cannot expect them to simply disappear. It is possible for your heart to carry your loved one and also love another. There is a unique ability to carry both experiences. There is a special place within us that carries the memories, the love and the experiences of the one we lost. However, it is okay and even expected to move forward toward a new love. The caution is to be sure you are moving forward and not trying to replace a lost love. The new person must be appreciated for who they are to you in your new phase. The new person needs the freedom to be who he or she is without the pressure of making you feel the same way you were with your first love. If you are not able to experience the new relationship without comparing the individual with your first love, it is very possible you are not ready to move forward.

Does this mean you will be forever wounded? No, but you will have a scar. Scars look very unbecoming at first, tender, inflamed, red and even glaring. But scars let us know that healing is taking place. I was wounded, but now I am healing. I have heard it said that when proper healing has taken place, and a scar has formed, the skin becomes stronger because it is made of fibers and not just skins cells.

What are the fibers that are strengthening my emotions?

> The Truth of God in my life
> The knowledge that I can trust God with my heart,
> my soul, my emotions
> The confidence that I have peace with God
> Healing oil over me
> The everlasting love of the Father
> Unexplainable joy
> Established identity
> Intimacy with God

These fibers hold me together. There is a song that Maverick City Music sings called "You Hold It All Together". He is the God of my present; He is the God of my future; He is in the middle; He holds it all together.

We can trust Him with each and every step, each and every moment. He allows us to trust Him in each area of our lives. We can trust Him with our hearts and emotions. We can trust Him for our healing. We can trust Him for our future. He is hiding you in the shadow of His wings. He is holding you in the palm of His hand. His strength is perfect when we are at our weakest. His words are life, His words are holy, but His words are also healing. He pours His fresh oil over you. He breathes His breath of life into you. He sustains you with HIS power, HIS anointing, HIS wisdom and HIS love. He is faithful, you can rely on Him. Receive His strength, take in His breath, and rest in His love.

The scripture in Psalms 23 where it says "He restores my soul", this is God restoring...

> the empty places
> the guarded places
> the broken places
> the lost dreams
> He is restoring all of you

I have seen over and again what restoration looks like. I have seen firsthand the beautiful stories of redemption. I have seen purity restored, marriages restored, health restored, mental health restored, families restored and Christian fellowship restored. These kinds of testimonies give others hope, renewed vision and new dreams. Your story is the hope for someone else's redemption and restoration.

"My glory and honor are fresh in me [being constantly renewed], and my bow gains [ever] new strength in my hand."
(Job 29:20 AMPC)

Let God heal you.
Let Him be your source and your strength.
During one of my lonely moments, the Lord gave me this message:

> Embrace where you are right now
> Embrace your independence
> Embrace your uniqueness
> You can do this with me
> I will still give you the desires of your heart

Just trust me right now
I'm not leaving you alone
When you need a personal touch, receive my embrace
When you need affection, receive mine

*"for I have learned in whatever state I am, to be content: I
can do all things through Christ who strengthens me."
(Philippians 4:11, 13 NKJV)*

*"Don't be pulled in different directions or worried about a thing. Be
saturated in prayer throughout each day, offering your faith-filled requests
before God with overflowing gratitude. Tell him every detail of your
life, then God's wonderful peace that transcends human understanding,
will make the answers known to you through Jesus Christ."
(Philippians 4:6-7 TPT)*

CHAPTER 4

Purity

"We have proved ourselves by our lifestyles of purity, by our
spiritual insights, by our patience, and by showing kindness, by
the Spirit of holiness and by our uncritical love for you."
(II Corinthians 6:6 TPT)

Naturally when we think of purity, we automatically think about our bodies. Living a life of purity certainly includes living a separated life that does not give in to the sensual desires of the flesh.

Don't look and lust

Don't commit adultery

Don't commit fornication

Don't have sex outside of marriage

Don't look at pornography

Don't dress like you are for sale

Don't tease

Don't touch

These are very good rules to follow. We should not do these things. Our physical purity is extremely important in living our lives for Christ. It is also important to our own development as an individual. How we treat our bodies and allow our bodies to be treated says so much about what we feel is true for ourselves and the God we serve. If we truly value ourselves in Christ, then we must hold fast to the fact that our bodies are the temple of the Holy Spirit. If we want the Holy Spirit to reside within us, we must keep His temple holy.

But let's take a step back....

Before we can truly be honest about our bodies and keep them pure, we must come face to face with the purity of our minds.

What is pure thinking?

Some find it funny that my entertainment goes only as far as a Hallmark or Pureflix movie or Christian fiction books. But this is how I keep my mind away from thoughts of physical intimacy or win the battle of temptations of the flesh. Would it be nice to be embraced once in a while by strong arms letting me know I am safe and secure? Would it be pleasant to receive a kiss on the cheek every now and then letting me know I am valued by someone? Yes and Yes! But if I dwell on these thoughts of what I am missing physically, they can quickly spin out of control. This is not the way for me to maintain purity. Yes, it is normal to be tempted. But I have the power given to me by God to resist the temptations and recognize the embrace of my Father when I need to feel safe and the sweet kiss of the Holy Spirit when I need to feel valued.

So purity is thinking good thoughts.

"Whatsoever things are true, whatsoever things are honest, whatsoever things are just, whatsoever things are pure, whatsoever things are lovely, whatsoever things are of good report; if there be any virtue, and if there be any praise, think on these things."
(Philippians 4:8 NKJV)

But is it more than that?

In Romans 12:3, Paul wrote "to think soberly" or "honestly assess your worth by using your God-given faith".

Thinking in our right mind...

Not allowing our thoughts to get away from us...

Not allowing ourselves to think more highly or more lowly...

One of my favorite scriptures, not because of the beautiful meaning, but because it holds me accountable, is II Corinthians 10:5 where Paul says to bring "every thought into captivity to the obedience of Christ". When thoughts come into my mind that do not agree with what Christ says or that are not uplifting or are disparaging, I speak this verse out loud. Some thoughts that come to distract, accuse or intimidate me are:

I am too old.

I am not beautiful.

I am too heavenly minded to be of any earthly good.

I am too outrageous.

I am too intense.

I bring these thoughts captive and I rewrite them through the lens of the Scripture and my relationship with Christ.

~~I am too old~~ I have experience with God that has come through my years!

~~I am not beautiful~~ I am lovely, there is no flaw in me!

~~I am too heavenly minded to be of any earthly good~~ I am kingdom minded!

~~I am too outrageous~~ I am living in freedom and liberty!

~~I am too intense~~ I am determined to live my life with purpose!

This is thinking soberly. This is bringing every thought captive. This is thinking with virtue and praise. This is purity in my mind.

Another thought about purity is that it starts in the spirit. When I received Christ as my personal Savior, my spirit was made pure and holy. It was not my purity, it was not my holiness. It was the purity of the spotless Lamb. It was the holiness of a righteous God.

My spirit is pure, because He is pure. I am a new creation because of what Christ did for me on the cross. My faith in God and the work of Jesus gave me a new spirit, a new heart.

When my heart is pure, my mind can be pure, and I can hold my body in purity. If I do not recognize the purity of my spirit, I will never conquer the purity of my mind and body.

I must recognize the beautiful work of Jesus made available to me by my Heavenly Father. Andrew Wommack speaks on this so beautifully in his book, *Spirit Soul and Body*. His teaching is so thorough and complete on this topic.

I no longer feel like I have to fight in my mind and body. I simply bring my mind and body into alignment with the finished work in my spirit. Simply – well, it sounds simple anyway. It is still an intentional action on my part.

Do I still struggle? Yes, but I now know how to fight these battles. I am not bound to my feelings, my emotions or distracting thoughts. I am not bound by my circumstances or memories. I am not bound by loss or disappointment. I am not bound by depression or disillusionment.

I am free! I am liberated! I am holy! I am a warrior! I am a daughter of the Most High God! I am healthy! I am whole!

"Create in me a clean heart, O God, and
renew a steadfast spirit within me."
(Psalm 51:10 NKJV)

"Keep creating in me a clean heart.
Fill me with pure thoughts and holy desires, ready to please you."
(Psalm 51:10 TPT)

There is also a purity of the Gospel. There are some things in the Word that we just need to receive. As one who was raised in a very conservative, Pentecostal denomination (and still in it), I have a tendency to read the Bible or hear a message and begin filtering it through the traditions of my upbringing, the doctrine of my denomination, my personal knowledge and my experiences. Many times I disqualify myself from receiving what God is saying because I am not able to balance it out with all my filters. But God's Word is more powerful than my filters.

For the word of God is living and powerful, and sharper than any two-edged sword, piercing even to the division of soul and spirit, and of joints and marrow, and is a discerner of the thoughts and intents of the heart.
(Hebrews 4:12 NKJV)

The two-edged sword is the Word of God. It pierces, it divides the emotions from the spirit that has been redeemed. It discerns not only our thoughts but why we are thinking them. It is living. It never dies. It is always relevant. It is powerful. It has the power to change the very nature of man, the very nature of me.

The Word of God is able to be all of these things because of the covenant God made with us. We are part of the new covenant. Jesus came. He was made flesh. John says that "the Word was made flesh and dwelt among us". He was the ultimate purity. He was the example of purity. John went on to say that "God so loved the world that He gave His only begotten Son, that whoever believes in Him should not perish but have everlasting life." This is the new covenant.

By grace.

We believe on Him who gave His life, who shed His blood. We participate in this covenant when we obey His word. This is the purest of covenants, made with the purest Lamb.

Let's look at purity of the Gospel from a different slant. When a warrior is armed with a sword, part of his armor is a sheath. A sheath is a protective covering for the sword. The sword cannot be tainted. It cannot be sullied. It must remain pure. The Word of God must remain pure, spotless. It cannot be remodeled to fit our personal theologies, our convenience or our feelings. The Word of God must remain sharp. It must retain its edge.

The sheath is also a protective covering for the warrior. It keeps the sword from wounding the warrior. The Word of God cannot harm the warrior because the warrior has taken care to properly tend to the Word of God. Paul calls it "rightly dividing the Word". Studying the Word of God while in relationship with the author maintains the purity of the Word.

> *...the Holy Spirit teaches, comparing spiritual things with spiritual.*
> *But the natural man does not receive the things of the*
> *Spirit of God, for they are foolishness to him; nor can he*
> *know them, because they are spiritually discerned.*
> *(I Corinthians 2:12-14 NKJV)*

As I was preparing this chapter, I received this from a friend:

> We are the sheath. As we read the Word, we are polishing the sword and making it razor sharp making it ready to strike with lightning reflex, full of wisdom and knowledge. Our blows to the enemy have already been recorded and we're just fulfilling our destiny. You are a vital part of our ministry. You lead with caution being sure what you say and do is of God and not of your flesh. You seek out the truth and align all with His Word. You look not just for the fruit, but at its root. God knows your heart and is still entrusting you

with more. There is a seed of discernment buried deep inside you that is taking root. The more you seek out the desires of healing, the more this seed will spring forth in you.

I am very aware of how I handle the Word of God in my life. I am also very intentional in how I minister and walk out my calling. There has to be a purity of heart to ensure I do not taint or tarnish the goodness that God wants me to share with others. If my motives are not pure, then I can easily take advantage of those I am to love.

Purity is multi-faceted and it is almost impossible to maintain without the Holy Spirit to teach me. I need God my Father. I need Jesus my Savior. I need the Holy Spirit my Comforter. I need the Word of God. Purity of my mind, body and spirit and the way the Word of God is applied to my life can only be attained through my intimacy with God.

CHAPTER 5

Good Grief

Grieving is not for those who are gone. It is for us who are still here. Grief is how we reconcile our memories. It is how we adjust to life without our loved ones. It is how we manage our emotions. It is how we learn to move forward. Grief is how we reconsider our expectations.

Grief is a natural and necessary part of life. We have to process loss, either through death, divorce or abandonment. It is essential to allow this to work through our lives. There is no denying it. If you try to put it off, it will show up eventually, when you least expect it, in an unusual place or circumstance. You will grieve, like it or not.

There is also a great deal of difference between good grief and bad grief. I suppose it would be better to say, healthy grief and unhealthy grief. I know the difference…I have lived it.

I am the youngest girl in our family of twelve children. I always believed I was my father's favorite. I later learned that each of us felt that same way. Dad had a unique and beautiful way of making each one feel very special, incredibly loved and extremely talented.

When my father went to be with Jesus, we had just learned that my husband's cancer had come back. My husband was going to preach my father's funeral in Knoxville, Tennessee, then we would go directly to Duke Cancer Center in Durham, North Carolina, for my husband to receive radiation treatments as the months of chemotherapy had not completed the job.

It was too much for me. My dad was my best friend. He taught me how to play Rook, volleyball and softball. He taught me how to be a fan not just a spectator. He taught me what it meant to be patriotic. He taught me how to play the organ and piano. He taught me how to harmonize. He taught me how to study. He taught me how to teach. He taught me how to minister and serve. He taught me how to live in forgiveness, compassion, integrity, faithfulness, love and kindness. He was the closest person I have ever known that resembled the nature of Father God. He was an incredible man. My father was the one who was the most concerned about how I was handling my husband's illness. My father always wanted to know how I was. Everyone else wanted to know about my husband (this was fine, it was important), but Dad cared about me too. I was not able to move forward when Dad left. During that time, I was grieving for Dad. I was grieving for my mother. I was grieving my marriage. I was grieving our pastoral ministry. I was over my head in grief.

I walked in that terrible grief for over three years. It was an awful time to get through life. I felt like I was losing my mind on some days. Other days, I could not find any joy. I questioned everything. I had a hard time making decisions. I had difficulty working. I changed jobs. I used to travel for work, I then began working from home. It seemed there was never any let up in responsibilities or decisions. I felt so alone. There was no one to share my grief. No one understood my feelings of darkness. No one knew how overwhelming all of it was. I was drowning, and I was not sure I wanted to come back up.

I finally found healing for my soul, rest for my body and peace in my spirit. It was a beautiful time of healing sitting on a church pew with no pastoral duties, no ministry title and no close friends. Jesus met me, poured in the healing oil, embraced me and lavished His love on me.

When my husband died, I had one question. Why did I have to be the first widow among our family and friends? Yes, my mother was a widow, but Mom was in a memory care facility not knowing who I was or any of our family. I felt like I was the first one to face it straight on. I had no model to follow. I had no one to show me how to react, respond or recover.

My husband was a great man. His charisma and intensity won me over in the very beginning. He gave 150% in everything he did. His singing, his preaching, his encouragement, his love, his intimacy, his grace, his faithfulness, his serving, his pastoring, his worship, his fathering, his cheerleading – everything was over the top. James was loud, boisterous and noticed, but he was also contemplative, loving and kind. He was the most generous person I have ever known. Seeing him in pain, discontentment and frustration was one of the most difficult things to watch as his wife of over 35 years. He did not deserve the suffering. He did not deserve the abbreviation in his life. He deserved to see his youngest son get married. He deserved to see the newest grandbabies. He deserved to see his grandsons grow to be strong, godly men. He deserved to see his granddaughters grow to be amazing, godly women. He deserved to stay and grow old with me. But our journey changed so much. I grieved the man I knew. I grieved the man he had become due to disease. I grieved what he would miss. I grieved what my children and grandchildren would miss. I grieved losing him.

But although it has been a journey into the unknown, this grief for my husband has been healthier. Trust me, it is there, it is real, it is painful and some days overwhelming. But this grief is not suffocating me. I can get through the days. I can allow the tears and the rush of memories at random moments. I hear a song, see a man walking with a cane, glimpse a familiar book, wear a particular piece of jewelry, watch an old show, glance at the grocery shelf, hear a certain sound, go to a specific store, and on and on and on it goes.

My husband always prayed for me and our children. I knew I was covered in prayer every single day. Even when he was in pain, in the hospital, receiving treatments, not having a good day, he prayed… for me. I was aware of this not long after his passing. I felt like I was aimlessly wandering around. I knew something significant was missing. If you have never experienced this kind of relationship, you don't know what you're missing. If you are familiar with this, you know exactly what I'm talking about. Almost two years after my husband's death, I was faced with a difficult situation in ministry. Not only was it a difficult hit, but I profoundly missed the prayer covering. I needed wisdom, understanding, strength, support…. I didn't feel comfortable asking anyone else to replace this act of love and devotion. I couldn't just ask someone. A dear friend of mine reassured me that I was not walking alone in this area of ministry; I had the prayers and support of several who were close to me…. But I missed my husband's prayers. He knew my weaknesses. He knew my strengths. He knew how to motivate me.

I used to say to God, "Let him know I miss him". But why would God relay that message? To make him feel guilty for leaving? Why did I feel compelled to share how much I missed him? He used to say, "You're the greatest woman in the world!", but I had so much angst with all of the decisions, caregiving, doctor visits, meal planning and also frustration, rejection, abandonment, anger, resentment. I was afraid I had not shown him enough how much I cared while he was here. I was afraid he did not know how much I really did love him, and still do. I was afraid I had not done enough, loved enough, cared enough, prayed enough…I was not enough. When I finally resolved that I was not why he died, he did not hate me, I really did do my best…When I finally understood the unconditional love, the matchless grace, the unending mercy of a most loving Father, I was able to let the grief subside and life became more manageable.

Grieving can come to a close sooner (at least the overwhelming part of it) when we accept our actions and forgive ourselves. It is better to face it and reconcile all the feelings than try to fight them, ignore them or deny them. Grief, when embraced in a healthy way, can be a beautiful healing process.

I was pulling out some boxes in my closet and came across some items I had kept of my parents and my husband. My first reaction was, "Is this all I have left of who you were to me?" I was quickly reminded that a legacy is not found in a box in a closet, a shrine in the room or even in a will. The legacy is found in the baptism of my grandson, the dedication of my granddaughter, the ministries of my children, the worship that resounds in each of their homes, the desire not only to see our loved ones in Heaven but to live out the callings and the giftings passed on through the generations. Yes, I have mementos of wonderful loved ones, but I also see them living through each of those they touched when they were here on earth. I am consciously aware of my blessings, yesterday's, today's and those on the way.

I was given an orchid plant last year. I don't have a green thumb. I was convinced I had killed it when the blooms went away. A friend of mine assured me it wasn't dead. I saw yesterday it had buds. I saw today there was a bloom. Remembering a great man, feeling the loss, then seeing that life does bloom again.

Even when you think all inside you is dead not just from the loss of a loved one but any kind of loss. Keep watering your spirit with worship and the Word. Keep your head toward the Son. You will bloom again.

It may come when you're trying to remember your grief and pain, but God says to divert your attention to the living.

I remember a great man but I look at our grandchildren who are walking in his example of loving Jesus, being bold in their testimonies, praying with faith, worshipping with exuberance, caring for others... remembering the old (previous, former) but being sure to focus on the new.

> *"Because of the Lord's great love we are not*
> *consumed, for his compassions never fail.*
> *They are new every morning; great is your faithfulness.*
> *I say to myself, "The Lord is my portion; therefore I will wait for him."*
> *The Lord is good to those whose hope is in him, to the one who seeks him;"*
> *(Lamentations 3:22-25 NIV)*

CHAPTER 6

In everything, really??

There are so many who are knee-deep in the struggles of life. There are those who feel they are being strangled with life's situations. If you have been asking these questions:

Where is God?

What am I doing?

How can I make it?

Or you feel like:

It's too hard...

It's not fair...

I'm hurting...

It's time for thanksgiving.

Paul said "In everything give thanks ..." He said IN not FOR. I was listening to this song by Maverick City Music and the following words caught my attention:

You sang 'til I found my song
You danced 'til my heart woke up
Now I move to the rhythm of love
I can't praise You enough

You wept 'til I found my strength
You lost Your breath dying to save me
Now I'll never go back to that grave
I can't praise You enough
(Thank You lyrics © Emi Blackwood Music Inc)

The revelation of this song is so rich to me. HE sang. HE danced. HE wept. HE lost His breath. Sometimes I feel like I have to make it all happen. But knowing that HE is doing the work until I am able; to see that it is HE who is pulling me back together. It is HE who is propping me up. It is HE who is building me and rebuilding me. It is HE who is washing over me with His love, His kindness and His grace.

One of the hardest things to do in the midst of a trial or difficult situation is to be thankful. With clean hands and a pure heart, be thankful. But the song lyrics remind us that God is with us always, in the midst of, right with us in the place of our hardship.

Let Him hold you up until you find your footing. Let Him carry you until you find your strength. He is there for you, with you and in you ~

Hebrews talks about a great cloud of witnesses who are in heaven rooting us on. These are family members, friends, loved ones...Paul also talked about those who are here supporting us now, praying for us here and now.

I am so thankful for my children who give me strength; who don't let me whine or complain, but they challenge me to take it up a notch. They help me pray about things. They release words of encouragement, motivation, healing and wisdom. They choose words of life, not condemnation. They make me laugh~

I am also thankful for my siblings who, though far away, support me, pray for me and encourage me. I love that I can call on any one of them and hear laughter and joy!

I am thankful for close friends who give me a safe place to release my cares, insecurities and frustrations. Their mere presence means so much. Sometimes it's a meal, a walk, a prayer, other times it's a hug, a laugh, or a word of encouragement ... EVERY time it is a transfer of strength, peace, joy and love that carries me to the next step of faith.

I have learned that this walk of faith should not be done alone, but with family and friends who love and support you. Reach out to others, whether you think you need them or they need you...you actually need each other.

"As for us, we have all of these great witnesses who encircle us
like clouds. So we must let go of every wound that has pierced
us and the sin we so easily fall into. Then we will be able to
run life's marathon race with passion and determination,
for the path has been already marked out before us."
(Hebrews 12:1 TPT)

"as you labor together with us through prayer. Because there
are so many interceding for us, our deliverance will cause
even more people to give thanks to God. What a gracious
gift of mercy surrounds us because of your prayers!"
(2 Corinthians 1:11 TPT)

CHAPTER 7

Transition. Shift.

In transitional periods of life, there are times when we just need to recalibrate.

I had to sell our townhouse one month after my husband's passing. It was a necessity, not a whim. When I moved from my home, friends, family and previous church members were there to help me pack my belongings in the storage unit. I am thankful for those who were there during that time.

After that I stayed with my daughters for weeks at a time. I was so fortunate to have a job that I could do from anywhere. I worked in Virginia. I worked in Texas. I even worked at Hilton Head!

Reality was closing in. I had to handle financial affairs, complete cemetery arrangements, and decide where I was going to live geographically. Because God had already set me up so beautifully in a church with friends and ministry opportunities, it was almost easy to decide the geographic area.

After a full three months of handling only what was absolutely required, allowing my children to pamper me, play with my grandchildren any time I wanted, I moved into a small apartment... alone. When I moved my belongings from the storage unit to my new apartment, friends, strong men, ministry team members, and pastors from my new church family were on hand in remarkable numbers.

That one decision – where to live – was all I could handle. No one understands the overwhelming flow of emotions unless they have experienced it. I probably had it so much easier than many. But it was so hard. When you are not used to making decisions just for yourself, it seems so easy to say, "Hey, I can get what I want". But now you have to know what you want. It is not that we can be so waffling or indecisive. It is more that we have always considered someone else. That is a good thing. The Bible says to prefer another. It is the shift that has to take place in the brain that says, it is no longer an option to consider anyone else in the home. No one else is there to give input. No one else is there to care about it. No one else is there to say it doesn't matter. No one else is there.

The dynamics are so different when you have to learn how to live alone, especially when it was not your choice to live alone. I want my option back! I want to share ideas again. I want to talk about our dreams again. I want someone else to decide.

I feel like a child, running to his mother, saying "Look, what I did!" I feel like I now go to my kids for their affirmation, their motivation, their love and acceptance. I want them to say "Wow, Mom, you did good." Because I overcame a hurdle in my life. Because I adapted. Because I recovered from the hit. Because I can say what color I want. Because I can say where I want to live. Because I can make a decision on my own. Because I want to matter to someone.

What do people do without God to take their every care and disappointment to? What do people do without children who can pick up the pieces of a widowed parent and help them take the next step? What do people do without community, friends, who walk through the challenges of moving, times of deep grieving, moments of erratic emotions, and surround them with support and love?

While in worship one Sunday, I clearly heard the word "transition", then "shift". Yes, I had been transitioning for a little while but SHIFT let me know it's time to pivot for something new, an acceleration to another place, a clear vision on expectation.

What's next? I don't know. But here's what I DO know. He said He would never leave me. He said He would move the obstructions and cut out the path that I am to take.

Here's to the exciting adventure of walking by faith, living the Kingdom life and experiencing the greater~

"Never doubt God's mighty power to work in you and accomplish all this. He will achieve infinitely more than your greatest request, your most unbelievable dream, and exceed your wildest imagination! He will outdo them all, for his miraculous power constantly energizes you."
(Ephesians 3:20 TPT)

I don't always understand what is happening at the time it is happening. I have tried not to overthink every situation. It is the challenge of learning to trust God and walk by faith in confidence.

What does it mean to lay down my life? Collins Dictionary states that "if someone lays down their life for another person, they die so that the other person can live." If I am laying down my life, I am dying to myself, my carnal nature, so that Jesus can live through me. If my ways are overshadowing His ways, I am not laying down my life. If my characteristics do not look like His characteristics, I am not laying down my life. John 3:20 says "He must increase, but I might decrease". He should be living through me in such a way that you can only see me through Him.

What does it mean to challenge my own desires? Psalm 37:4 says

"Delight yourself also in the Lord, and He shall give you the desires of your heart". He can give us our desires if we delight in Him first. When we delight in Him first, His desires become our desires. Just as in a romantic or intimate relationship, we constantly want to fulfill the desires of the one we love. It is not what I want to eat, what do you want? It is not where I want to go, where do you want to go? It is not what I want to see, what do you want to see? The focus moves from me to the one I delight in. My desires are now what He desires.

What does it mean to sit quietly and just hear Him speak? I have been so guilty of being busy. Busy doing mostly good things. Busy doing mostly the expected things. Busy doing anything to keep my mind occupied. I feel as though I am not good on my own without being busy. This is why when God wants to speak to me, He usually does so right before I am ready to fall asleep or just as I am rousing to wake. My mind is not focused elsewhere, He can actually get a word in. I am learning to sit. I am learning to be in the car without the radio. I am learning to be in the house without the TV or music playing. I am learning how to be quiet and let Him speak. Sometimes I will say, "Lord, what do you want to say to me today? I am listening."

What does it look like to walk where He leads? I could never have planned my life the way it is turning out. I got married at the age of 19. I thought my marriage would last forever. We started fulltime ministry when I was 29. I thought I would be a pastor's wife forever. I have been in music ministry as a musician and/or worship leader since I was 14. I thought this would be forever. It was never on my radar to be the director of a supernatural school of ministry. It was never on my radar to be one who works in deliverance. It was never on my radar to lead a healing ministry. All I knew was that I wanted more of God. I wanted to see greater things. I wanted to be in the middle of what God was doing. Walking where He leads does not mean you will always know where you are going. Most of the time it is a walk of faith.

I admit it. I don't always know the answers to life's questions. I don't know the answers to ministry questions. Many times I just don't know. I know what truth is. I know what trust in God is. I know the faithfulness of God. I know that God knows more about how to live my life than I do. I know that God does what God does and I am better off doing what He is doing. I do not always know the answers.

I do know when I am not walking in peace. I do know when I am not living in joy. I do know when I am not enjoying my place in life. I prefer peace. I prefer joy. I prefer abundant life.

CHAPTER 8

The Problem with Joy

Webster's Dictionary 1828 defines joy "as the passion or emotion excited by the acquisition or expectation of good; that excitement of pleasurable feelings which is caused by success, good fortune, the gratification of desire or some good possessed, or by a rational prospect of possessing what we love or desire; gladness; exultation; exhilaration of spirits. Joy is a delight of the mind, from the consideration of the present or assured approaching possession of a good. A glorious and triumphant state."

All throughout scripture, joy is shown with resistance.

"My brethren, count it all joy when you fall into various trials"
(James 1:2 NKJV)

Who wants to have joy in the midst of trials? Aren't we supposed to whine, complain and pout? James said count it JOY! It sounds like a choice in perspective~

"Then the angel said to them, "Do not be afraid, for behold, I bring you good tidings of great joy which will be to all people."
(Luke 2:10 NKJV)

This is just as strange...don't be afraid, I brought you JOY for everyone! We are to bring forth JOY even through the things we fear.

What are we afraid of?	Being alone = JOY
	Social unrest = JOY
	Political chaos = JOY
	Sickness = JOY
	Financial insecurity = JOY
	Failure = JOY

"whom having not seen you love. Though now you do not see Him,
yet believing, you rejoice with joy inexpressible and full of glory,"
(I Peter 1:8 NKJV)

We should have joy while we wait...waiting on unanswered prayers... waiting on the prodigal to come home...waiting on healing...waiting on financial breakthrough...waiting on marital issues to be resolved. While we wait, we should rejoice with JOY!

"Those who sow in tears shall reap in joy."
(Psalms 126:5 NKJV)

Even our pain and suffering should produce joy. Even when lonely days are endless. Even when grief has overtaken us. Even when strife has come in. Even when ~ there is JOY!

In my ministry with women and helping them to understand who they are in Christ, I have prayed for them to receive their ROAR. In the midst of struggles, difficult circumstances and trials, we have a tendency to do one of two things: complain or go silent. Believe it or not, the better option is to complain. Why complain? Because we still have our voice; we still have the ability to respond. Our voice has only been redirected. With our voice, we are not far from singing a song of victory, shouting a praise, expressing gratitude or simply crying tears of relief. We are not too far gone that we cannot see the good that is coming.

There are times in our lives that are more extreme. Deep loss, extraordinary hardships, dark circumstances, abuses and victim situations can leave us with a heavy weight of guilt, shame, loneliness, rejection and an inability to respond. These extremes in life can choke us, take our voice, diminish our expression, and inhibit our reaction.

It has been said that apathy is the worse reaction to life. Too many times our circumstances strip us of our ability to react to life. We are not able to respond. We become voiceless; no one to hear, no one to care, no one to turn to. We lose our zest for life and our joy to live. In these times, we must allow God to restore our voice. We must allow Him to restore our emotions, even if it is painful at first. We must first FEEL, and then we can find our voice.

The problem with JOY is it is supposed to be in every situation, and it is a choice! We choose our attitude. We choose our perspective. We choose our response. We choose the condition of our heart. We can choose the Joy of the Lord.

The Joy of the Lord that is our strength!

The Joy of the Lord that will sustain us.

The Joy of the Lord that will keep us.

"The LORD has done great things for us, and we are filled with joy."
(Psalm 126:3 NKJV)

Choose JOY and roar with victory!

CHAPTER 9

Yes and Amen

There is great hope in the knowledge that God has already written my story. He knows the end from the beginning. Nothing has happened to me that God did not know was going to take place. I have learned that His grace goes before me every single time. There is no surprise for God. Although some things are not His perfect plan, all things are used for His good for us.

*"And we know that all things work together for **good** to those who love God, to those who are the called according to His purpose."*
(Romans 8:28 NKJV)

When my kids and I went to a Christian conference, several things were spoken to me.

First, God has heard every prayer I have spoken over my children. One person put it this way. She said I had planted an oak for each of my children. Although I let them make their own decisions as they grew older, I continued to water their oaks. Another told me that my children were arrows and each of them would hit the mark God had intended for them. One individual let me know that my specific prayers instrumented the change that birthed the beautiful, spiritual fruit in their lives.

God's faithfulness has been proven in each of their lives. Each of them carry a heavy anointing, great favor and a passion for Jesus. They raise their children in an atmosphere of worship and encountering God. They allow and expect dreams, visions, angelic encounters, signs and wonders.

The person who talked about the oaks I had planted for my children also told me that as I was watering the oaks for my children, God was watering mine. He was tending to me while I was tending to my family. One said that God is taking care of my future. I did not realize at the time of this word that I would need it so desperately.

One individual called me a Woman of Wonder. Little did I know then how much I would identify with the Wonder Woman image now. I have a bookshelf full of Wonder Woman paraphernalia. People bring me Wonder Woman items. It is a light joke with an element of truth around it. When I joke about being Wonder Woman, it is to remind myself of the strength and dignity that I carry because of my walk with Christ. It is also to remind me of the warrior spirit I carry for my family, my pastor, my church and my nation. I am a threat to the enemy because I know who I am.

I was told at that conference that I would prophesy. That gift was never a reality to me. It certainly is now. I was also given a phrase "Fire and three months". Nearly three months to the day, my pastor asked me to direct the satellite school of ministry to be hosted at our church. We started the school in September of 2018, and we are still going strong with a new group of students each year. Being part of discipling people into their identity in Christ, impartation of spiritual gifts, walking with them through evangelism and ministry is truly living in revival FIRE!

I have always thought it so beautiful and romantic for a husband and wife to dance together. This is not a reality that I have truly experienced. But one of the prophetic words I received was that God was inviting me into a place of awe and wonder. He was inviting me to dance with Him. I think this is one of those God-winks where He knows the desires of my heart and speaks to those specific desires that I have never vocalized to anyone. What a revelation to know that moments with God are not to be stressful, rigid and religious but they are to be a time of intimacy, love and freedom.

This song was sung over me:

WE DANCE

You steady me

Slow and sweet we sway

Take the lead and I will follow

Finally ready now

To close my eyes and just believe

That you won't lead me where you don't go

When my faith gets tired

And my hope seems lost

You spin me round and round

And remind me of that song

The one you wrote for me

And we dance ~ And we dance ~ And we dance ~ And we dance

And I will lock eyes

With the one who's ransomed me

The one who gave me joy from mourning

And I will lock eyes

With the one who's chosen me

The one who set my feet to dancing

There are so many other promises, words of revelation and dreams that God has given to me through my personal conversations with God, words from friends, revelation from strangers and encouragement from family. I know beyond the shadow of a doubt that I am protected, provided for, carried, loved and strengthened all my days. I never need to fear, be in anxiety or feel intimidated because I know I am a daughter of God.

> *"For all the promises of God in Him are Yes, and in*
> *Him Amen, to the glory of God through us."*
> *(II Corinthians 1:20 NKJV)*

CHAPTER 10

The Story I'll Tell

"Imagine yourself as a living house. God comes in to rebuild that house. At first, perhaps, you can understand what He is doing. He is getting the drains right and stopping the leaks in the roof and so on; you knew that those jobs needed doing and so you are not surprised. But presently He starts knocking the house about in a way that hurts abominably and does not seem to make any sense. What on earth is He up to? The explanation is that He is building quite a different house from the one you thought of - throwing out a new wing here, putting on an extra floor there, running up towers, making courtyards. You thought you were being made into a decent little cottage: but He is building a palace. He intends to come and live in it Himself."
- C.S. Lewis, Mere Christianity

My favorite movie is "It's a Wonderful Life" with Jimmy Stewart. During a particularly hard spot in my life, my daughter, Anna, bought me a journal with this as the title on the cover. I wrote a great deal in that book. It was a reminder that regardless of what is going on around me, my life is wonderful. I have incredible, amazing children. Their spouses are even amazing! I have beautiful, fun, energetic grandchildren. I was married to a very good man for almost 36 years.

Because it is a wonderful life, I do not live from a place of loss. Don't get me wrong. Loss is real. Pain is real. Trauma is real. But my identity comes from the rest of my story, not from a moment in time, not even a moment that changed my life forever. Once I saw only illness, depression, anxiety, hopelessness and despair, but now I see with a sense of WONDER. I see the healing in my life, the restoring of my soul, the opening of my eyes to the beauty around me, the everyday blessings.

I live intentionally. I breathe with purpose. I serve with humility. I believe that since I was left here on this earth without my lifelong partner and mate, then I was meant to be here. I was not left here to be stuck in grief. I was not left here to wallow in my self-pity. I was not left here to wander around aimlessly. I have a life to live that may even impact someone else.

I see the pain that others carry. I understand their grief all too well. But I personally do not live there anymore. It was a passing visitation. Just like my little apartment was for a brief stay, so is the time to put my life on hold and grieve. Widow may describe my marital status but it does not dictate my life. I have lost a partner for life on this earth. I miss him every single day. There are moments it is difficult to breathe because of his absence. But I have not lost him for eternity. I know exactly where he is and I know where I am going one day.

In the midst of this life of being "independent", "single", "a lone ranger", God has proven Himself to me over and over and over again. Not long after my husband's passing, the song "Goodness of God" became popular. When we sang it at church, I would just cry. I would zone in on the lyrics that said "I love Your voice. You have led me through the fire. In the darkest night You are close like no other." Then the song would say, "And all my life You have been faithful. And all my life You have been so, so good." I would weep over the faithfulness of God. I would melt in the love of a Father who sees me. The bridge to the song says, "His goodness is running after me". In spite of where I am in my emotions, in my grief, in my loneliness, in my widowhood, in my circumstances, the goodness of God is chasing after me! I cannot escape His goodness! I cannot escape His blessings or His favor! It is the goodness of God that keeps me moving~

After my first year of being a widow, my ministry class students gave me a necklace. One of the charms has one word on it "Seen". Later in the same week that I received the necklace, I received a card that had the scripture in Genesis 16:13 that talks about "You-Are-the-God-Who-Sees". God sees me. He saw me then. He sees me now. His eyes are watching over me. Psalm 91 in the NKJV says, "He shall cover you with His feathers, and under His wings you shall take refuge; His truth shall be your shield and buckler." The Passion Translation says it this way, "His massive arms are wrapped around you, protecting you. You can run under his covering of majesty and hide. His arms of faithfulness are a shield keeping you from harm."

I do not have to fear. I do not have to be alone. I do not have to be concerned for my provision. I do not have to worry about the cares of this world. I need only lean into the strong arm of my Father. I can rest knowing that He will be my defender. He will be my husband. He will be my provider. He will be my protector.

> *"A father of the fatherless, a defender of widows,*
> *Is God in His holy habitation."*
> *(Psalms 68:5 NKJV)*

> *"He will establish the boundary of the widow."*
> *(Proverbs 15:25 NKJV)*

I live my life with purpose. I purpose to partner with God and do what He does. I want my heart to be in rhythm with His heart. I am learning how to hear His voice above all other voices. I am being intentional in how I live life.

I do have to be careful that I am not busy for the sake of being busy. Busyness looks like responsibility disguised as distraction. There have been times, and still are every now and again, where it is hard for me to be by myself for more than a couple of hours. My mind whirls with what-ifs, why-didn't-I, I-can't, I'm-not…. I have to shift gears and take these thoughts captive and replace them with the truth of God. What-if thoughts have no value. Why-didn't-I thoughts are not constructive. I-can't thoughts are helpless. I'm-not thoughts are hopeless. These do not build up what God is building up in me. I have to recognize that although life, ministry, work, play and family is all different now, it is still good…very good.

There is a loss but there is also great gain. I am living life with boldness and intentionality. Before I was withdrawn, not very social and did what was expected. I have begun ministering in a fresh, new way. Before I ministered the way my husband directed me to do or gave me opportunity. I am seeing how limitless God's plans are for me. Before I felt the plans were for my husband and I was to follow those plans. As I take one step with God, He opens the pathway for another step.

I heard an illustration once a very long time ago. The headlights on a car will shine from Virginia to Ohio; however, you cannot sit in your car in Virginia and see Ohio. But as you take the journey the headlights will guide your way all the way to your destination.

I may not see the fullness of my destination right now but I can trust that God will lead me each step of the way, each leg of the journey. I am confident that He who has begun a good work in me will complete it. I am not put aside while I grieve. God can use me while I am healing. I serve through the pain to get me through to the other side. As I understand where I am in the process of grief and healing, I can better see the process in someone else. I would never presume to think that all who have lost a spouse or loved one grieve the same way I do. However, there are similarities in the process. All situations are different. All circumstances vary according to the relationships of the husband and wife and their relationship to God. I knew of the faithfulness of God prior to my husband's illness. I learned a new aspect of God's faithfulness during his illness. I learned a whole new aspect of God's faithfulness following my husband's death. Men and women who have not had the history with God to know of His character before loss may not know what to expect of God after having experienced that loss.

One day as I was reading Psalms 61, "When my heart is overwhelmed…". I looked up the word "overwhelmed". It means to bury or drown beneath a huge mass, defeat completely, give too much of a thing to (someone); inundate, have a strong emotional effect on and be too strong for; overpower. Two of these definitions stood out to me. Defeat completely and be too strong for; overpower. When my heart is overwhelmed with pain, insecurity, shame, fear, grief, betrayal or loneliness… I can feel defeated completely. I can feel overpowered. It's too much for the human heart to contend with. When any of these emotions or situations take over, any of us can without fail be most miserable.

Being overwhelmed brings to mind a waterfall, gushing down over the wall, overpowering everything in its path… it's like when a dam breaks and the water is released to go wherever it wants. There is nothing in the natural that can stop the force of the water; you either move out of its way or you succumb to its power.

But when my heart is overwhelmed…when I can't take it anymore… when I am no longer able to process…LEAD ME TO THE ROCK! The Rock is stable, the Rock is secure, the Rock will not be moved. Lead me there…to the ROCK! When life has taken over and I'm not able to resist the weight, the burden, the heaviness, I can go to the rock that will not give way.

Emotional healing can be messy – silent tears, crying, screaming, brokenness, pleading- As much as emotions are from God, they can get away from me and try to dictate my response to life. I have a strong tendency to put up walls. I like to hide behind my defense mechanisms. I even run from people. But God strips away the pain one layer at a time. He removes the walls from my heart. He reasons with me regarding my defense mechanisms. He has me minister to others in need. He loves me enough not to leave me where I am. This is not just sin, but it is also my brokenness.

How do I bring healing to others if I am still in a state of brokenness? It's not impossible to minister to others in this brokenness. But that is not the best place to minister from. God would have me be healed, whole and free. He would have me minister from a place of overflow, not a place of barely enough. Even as I write these very words, I can sense His overwhelming love rushing over my mind. I can feel His strength inside me. I am able to relax and rest in Him because He has led me, is leading me and will continue to lead me into healing and wholeness.

> *"Give careful attention to your spiritual life and every cherished truth you teach, for living what you preach will then release even more abundant life inside you and to all those who listen to you."*
> *(1 Timothy 4:16 TPT)*

Much of my healing has taken place through people God has put in my life. It is not just my children, grandchildren and siblings, but it is also through friends. I have never experienced such friendship before. I have learned the importance of community. I know why friendship is so significant. One of my dear friends gave me this word from the Lord on the second anniversary of my husband's passing:

I am turning a new chapter in your life and healing the pain.
I am restoring the years the canker worm and locusts have eaten.
I will use you to speak hope to the hopeless and stir my gifts.
There is great fruit ahead of you.
Remember you are Mine and I am always with you.

What a blessed hope! I know that intimacy with God is my lifeline in this world. I live to see the greatness of God. I desire to be part of what God is doing and celebrate His goodness.

It is not surprising to know that God knew ahead of time that this is the place I would be today. It is also not surprising to know that He had already made promises to me. I stand on these promises. I trust these promises because I can trust the God who made them.

""Do not fear, for you will not be ashamed; Neither be disgraced,
for you will not be put to shame; For you will forget the shame of
your youth, and will not remember the reproach of your widowhood
anymore. For your Maker is your husband, The LORD of hosts is
His name; and your Redeemer is the Holy One of Israel; He is called
the God of the whole earth. For the LORD has called you like a
woman forsaken and grieved in spirit, like a youthful wife when you
were refused," Says your God. "For a mere moment I have forsaken
you, but with great mercies I will gather you. With a little wrath I
hid My face from you for a moment; But with everlasting kindness
I will have mercy on you," Says the LORD, your Redeemer."
(Isaiah 54:4-8 NKJV)

"For He shall give His angels charge over you,
To keep you in all your ways."
(Psalms 91:11 NKJV)

"The Lord watches over the foreigner and sustains the fatherless and the widow, but he frustrates the ways of the wicked."
(Psalms 146:9 NIV)

"He offers a resting place for me in his luxurious love. His tracks take me to an oasis of peace near the quiet brook of bliss. That's where he restores and revives my life. He opens before me the right path and leads me along in his footsteps of righteousness so that I can bring honor to his name. Even when your path takes me through the valley of deepest darkness, fear will never conquer me, for you already have! Your authority is my strength and my peace. The comfort of your love takes away my fear. I'll never be lonely, for you are near."
(Psalms 23:2-4 TPT)

Day 1 of Encouragement

You are being released into a new freedom
of peace, joy and abundance
Abundance of grace, mercy, favor and blessing
You have so much to give
You feel as though your goodness has been
trampled ... and it has been
But do not look at what you see in the natural
Allow God to reveal to you what He sees
He sees your heart ~ He sees your motives ~ He sees your thoughts
He knows the intents of your thoughts
He loves you and is proud of you
It is only through His grace that He has released
His favor and blessing upon you
Go in His favor
See yourself sitting on His lap learning to be just like Him
Sit, take it all in, you won't get every characteristic
of your Father in one sitting
It takes time and time again
You are amazing
Not because you have arrived at perfection but because
you have chosen relationship over perfection
Sons and daughters learn to act like their
fathers in humility and grace
Carnal people try to become perfect by the world's
standards which are relative, not real
Enjoy the process ~

"For to which of the angels did He ever say: "You
are My Son, today I have begotten You"?
And again: "I will be to Him a Father, And He shall be to Me a Son"?
(Hebrews 1:5 NKJV)

"Stand fast therefore in the liberty by which Christ has made us
free, and do not be entangled again with a yoke of bondage."
(Galatians 5:1 NKJV)

Day 2 of Encouragement

I'm not surprised by disappointments
I'm not surprised when things don't go as you expected
Be still and know that I'm still God
Hear me when say I love you with an everlasting love
I called you, no one else did
Your calling, your destiny rests with me
I am with you through every step, every move
Don't look to men to satisfy
Look to me
Only I can do exceedingly abundantly
more than you can ask or think
Only I can provide for you
Only I can give you the blessings that come from Heaven
Only I can give you security
Look to me alone
I've not forgotten you
I'm setting you up for my purpose
Don't lose heart ~ Look to me

*"My fellow believers, when it seems as though you are
facing nothing but difficulties, see it as an invaluable
opportunity to experience the greatest joy that you can!
For you know that when your faith is tested it stirs
up power within you to endure all things.
And then as your endurance grows even stronger it will
release perfection into every part of your being until
there is nothing missing and nothing lacking.*

And if anyone longs to be wise, ask God for wisdom and he will give it!
He won't see your lack of wisdom as an opportunity to scold you over your
failures but he will overwhelm your failures with his generous grace.
Just make sure you ask empowered by confident faith without
doubting that you will receive. For the ambivalent person
believes one minute and doubts the next. Being undecided
makes you become like the rough seas driven and tossed by the
wind. You're up one minute and tossed down the next."
(James 1:2-6 TPT)

Day 3 of Encouragement

Come closer
Lay your head on my chest
Feel my heartbeat
Experience my love for you
I've given you beauty for ashes
You no longer have to ask if you measure up
I made you the way I wanted you to be
You are in my image
You are your Father's child
I can see Myself through your eyes
You have my characteristics
Let others see them

"To grant [consolation and joy] to those who mourn in Zion—to give them an ornament (a garland or diadem) of beauty instead of ashes, the oil of joy instead of mourning, the garment [expressive] of praise instead of a heavy, burdened, and failing spirit—that they may be called oaks of righteousness [lofty, strong, and magnificent, distinguished for uprightness, justice, and right standing with God], the planting of the Lord, that He may be glorified."
(Isaiah 61:3 AMPC)

Day 4 of Encouragement

You have battled with what you should do next.
The Father says He has been preparing you for your destiny but
you have not yet trusted Him with every part of your life.
His will for you will bring you peace which you have been longing for.
His plan will give you hope that you have been afraid to embrace.
His purpose will give you the future with the
security of protection and provision.

Call on Him~
He's waiting for you~
Your life is to bring Him glory~
Come to Him~
He's ready to respond~

*"For I know the thoughts that I think toward you, says the
LORD, thoughts of peace and not of evil, to give you a future
and a hope. Then you will call upon Me and go and pray
to Me, and I will listen to you. And you will seek Me and
find Me, when you search for Me with all your heart."
(Jeremiah 29:11-13 NKJV)*

Day 5 of Encouragement

And all I did was praise
All I did was worship
All I did was bow down, oh
All I did was stay still

Hallelujah, You have saved me
So much better Your way
Hallelujah, great Defender
So much better Your way
(**Defender:** *John-Paul Gentile, Steffany Gretzinger, and Rita Springer*)

One morning, these lyrics were resonating in my spirit.
There's something about being able to trust in God and
His goodness in the midst of chaos, storms and pain.
If I can keep my eyes on Him and not my circumstances ...
If I can focus on who He is and not my inabilities or weaknesses ...
If I can turn my affections and adoration to
Him and not my fears and doubts ...
He fights for me!
He stands between me and the enemy!
He raises His banner over me!
He hides me in the shadow of His wings!
He walks with me!
He holds me up!
He provides, protects and heals!
He is my strength!
He is my joy!
He is my defender!

"He alone is my safe place; his wraparound presence always protects me. For he is my champion defender; there's no risk of failure with God. So why would I let worry paralyze me, even when troubles multiply around me?"

(Psalm 62:2 TPT)

Day 6 of Encouragement

When you think you can't take another step, He is there
When you feel your strength is waning, He is there
When you don't trust your own emotions, He is there
When you don't know what to do, He is there
When you are at your best, He is there
When you are at your worst, He is there

No matter your circumstances, He is with you
No matter your attitude, He is still there
When you feel abandoned, He never left you
When you feel cheated or wronged, it wasn't Him

How many times has He reminded you, "Be still and know..."?
How many times have you read of His faithfulness?
How many times have you experienced His
strength when you had none of your own?
He is closer than a brother ~ He cares more than you know

Don't be afraid ~ Be courageous
Don't get lost in negative emotions
Read and trust His promises

He knows your name ~ He has redeemed you ~ You are His
He does not ignore, disregard or disrespect
He loves, protects and provides

What a Friend We have in Jesus (Joseph
Scriven/Charles Crozat Converse)

Oh the Overwhelming, Never ending, **Reckless
Love of God** (Cory Asbury)
Great is Thy Faithfulness (Thomas Obediah
Chisholm/ William Marion Runyan)
He is **Alpha and Omega** (Erasmus Mutambira)
Jesus is the **Lover of My soul** (Steve Mcpherson,
John Ezzy & Daniel Grul)
Oh what peace ~ Oh what joy!

*"O Lord, You have searched me and known me.
You know my sitting down and my rising up;
You understand my thought afar off.
You comprehend my path and my lying down,
and are acquainted with all my ways.
For there is not a word on my tongue, but behold,
O Lord, You know it altogether.
You have hedged me behind and before, and laid Your hand upon me.
Such knowledge is too wonderful for me; it is high, I cannot attain it.
Where can I go from Your Spirit? Or where can I flee from Your presence?
If I ascend into heaven, You are there; If I make
my bed in hell, behold, You are there.
If I take the wings of the morning, and dwell
in the uttermost parts of the sea,
Even there Your hand shall lead me, and Your right hand shall hold me.
If I say, "Surely the darkness shall fall on me,"
Even the night shall be light about me;
Indeed, the darkness shall not hide from You, but the night shines
as the day; the darkness and the light are both alike to You.
For You formed my inward parts; You covered me in my mother's womb.*

I will praise You, for I am fearfully and wonderfully made;
marvelous are Your works, and that my soul knows very well.
My frame was not hidden from You, when I was made in secret,
and skillfully wrought in the lowest parts of the earth.
Your eyes saw my substance, being yet unformed. and
in Your book they all were written, the days fashioned
for me, when as yet there were none of them.
How precious also are Your thoughts to me, O
God! How great is the sum of them!
If I should count them, they would be more in number
than the sand; when I awake, I am still with You.
Oh, that You would slay the wicked, O God! Depart
from me, therefore, you bloodthirsty men.
For they speak against You wickedly; Your
enemies take Your name in vain.
Do I not hate them, O LORD, who hate You? And do
I not loathe those who rise up against You?
I hate them with perfect hatred; I count them my enemies.
Search me, O God, and know my heart; try me, and know my anxieties;
And see if there is any wicked way in me, and
lead me in the way everlasting."
(Psalm 139:1-24 NKJV)

Day 7 of Encouragement

He is going to redeem your memories
He is going to redeem your expectations
He is going to redeem your hope
He says that you ARE worthy to receive His blessings
You don't deserve any of God's goodness
God says No!
You are His and you deserve all the goodness because of His love
He is redeeming your gifts – The things you
have pushed away to punish yourself
He is redeeming your peace
All trauma is being broken now
All painful memories are being replaced now
When memories come, it will be your good times, not your bad ones
God is removing your pain
He is healing your broken heart
He is pouring in the oil of healing

"Though many wish to fight and the tide of battle turns against me,
by your power I will be safe and secure; peace will be my portion."
(Psalms 55:18 TPT)

Day 8 of Encouragement

My prayer

I desire to be one with You
I desire to be closer to You
I want to be close enough to hear Your voice
I want to be with You enough to obey Your voice
I want to know Your heart
I want my heart to be in time with Yours
I willingly lay down my life to be raised up again with You
I no longer want to be in the safe places
I want to be in the places that require me to risk
according to Your kingdom purposes
I want Your Fire to be around me and Your Glory to be in me

"As the deer pants for the water brooks, so pants my soul for You, O God."
(Psalm 42:1 NKJV)

"For I,' says the Lord, 'will be a wall of fire all around
her, and I will be the glory in her midst.'"
(Zechariah 2:5 NKJV)

Day 9 of Encouragement

You have wrestled with God
You have questioned not only His will but His ways
You have desired to know God more intimately but have
not been able to trust Him enough to fully let go
God desires for you to know Him intimately
He has great plans for you but it is necessary
for you to release everything to Him
It is time to release your desires to Him
It is time to release your fears, anxiety, insecurity and control to Him
He is ready to lead you ~ Be ready to follow
Your identity comes from Him and Him alone
Ask Him what He thinks about you
Ask Him how much He loves you
Ask Him what is next for you
Rest in Him
You have only scratched the surface in the
depth of relationship you have in Him
Just like Jacob, He wants to mark your life with a permanent stamp
He desires you to reclaim your identity
You have forgotten who He called you to be
You have forgotten that it was you, you
specifically, that He called to Himself
He longs for you to encounter Him in such a
way that your life will never be the same
He wants to bless you in such a way that your response is,
"I have seen God face to face, and my life is preserved"
He has saved your life
He had saved your relationships

He has protected you

He has preserved you

You may not have always understood what He was doing but be

assured that God does not withhold good things from His children

And you are one of His favorites

Get closer to Him

Snuggle up

Ask Him who He calls you for you "have struggled

with God and with men, and have prevailed"

"Then Jacob was left alone; and a Man wrestled
with him until the breaking of day.
And He said, "Let Me go, for the day breaks." But he
said, "I will not let You go unless You bless me!"
So He said to him, "What is your name?" He said, "Jacob." And He
said, "Your name shall no longer be called Jacob, but Israel; for you
have struggled with God and with men, and have prevailed."
Then Jacob asked, saying, "Tell me Your name, I pray." And He said,
"Why is it that you ask about My name?" And He blessed him there.
So Jacob called the name of the place Peniel: "For I have
seen God face to face, and my life is preserved."
Just as he crossed over Penuel the sun rose on
him, and he limped on his hip."
(Genesis 32:24, 26-31 NKJV)

Day 10 of Encouragement

Actively forgive as this releases God's blessings over you
Offer to the Lord your sacrifice even the sacrifice
of being wronged or treated unfairly
Forgive yourself ~ Forgive your thoughts against God
Shame must go and you no longer agree with feelings of unworthiness
The power of every negative word that has come
to you, from you or about you is cancelled
We release the identity of who God says He is
We release the mind of Christ
We release the overwhelming peace and
shalom that destroys the chaos
We release joy that gives strength
We release power, love and a sound mind

"Your own ears will hear him. Right behind you a voice will say,
"This is the way you should go, whether to the right or to the left."
(Isaiah 30:21 NLT)

"For the LORD God is a sun and shield; The LORD will give grace and
glory; No good thing will He withhold from those who walk uprightly."
(Psalms 84:11 NKJV)

"Never doubt God's mighty power to work in you and accomplish all
this. He will achieve infinitely more than your greatest request, your
most unbelievable dream, and exceed your wildest imagination! He will
outdo them all, for his miraculous power constantly energizes you."
(Ephesians 3:20 TPT)

Do not look at the natural ~ God is working in the
spiritual ~ It will manifest in the natural

Be still and know ~ God is working things out for His good
His purposes in you and His destiny for you will not be dismissed
They will come to fruition
The desires you have had before are not forgotten or delayed

There is a shift – A shift in perspective – A shift toward
boldness – A shift toward trust – A shift toward
rest - A shift in expectation and anticipation

"Surrender your anxiety. Be still and realize that I am God. I am God
above all the nations, and I am exalted throughout the whole earth."
(Psalm 46:10 TPT)

Day 11 of Encouragement

Don't let it be said of us that we did not know that the Lord is in this place... in this very place... in this very time... in this very moment

God has not left us ~ He is among us
God has not forgotten us ~ He is with us
God has not abandoned us ~ He is fighting for us

We are peering into the portal of Heaven
We are witnessing the mighty power of God
In the midst of these dark and dreary days, I have
seen healings, deliverances, people filled with the
Holy Spirit, people encountering God

"Surely the LORD is in this place"
Be sure you know it

Don't be distracted
Don't be alarmed
Do not fear
The Lord is here

One song says it this way...
"Let us become more aware of your presence; Let
us experience the glory of your goodness"
(**Holy Spirit**: Bryan and Katie Torwalt)

*"Then Jacob awoke from his sleep and said, "Surely the
LORD is in this place, and I did not know it."
And he was afraid and said, "How awesome is this place! This is
none other than the house of God, and this is the gate of heaven!""*
(Genesis 28:16-17 NKJV)

Day 12 of Encouragement

Father, why is it difficult for me to believe
that in your love, I am complete?
Why do I feel like I must perform, stay busy, work
at living for you in being the right example?

My will is rest for you
My will is peace and joy for you
My yoke is easy, and my burden is light
When you accepted me, I accepted you
My acceptance of you was not conditional upon your performance
I received you as you are
Any work you do for me should be out of love and
appreciation, not guilt or condemnation
Learn to trust that there is nothing you can do to earn my love
Learn to trust that I am not waiting on your performance
I want you to walk beside me
Partner with me, don't perform for me
Receive my love without restraint
Receive my love without conditions
You are complete in me, not in you
Your completion comes through my love to you

Come to Me, all you who labor and are heavy
laden, and I will give you rest.
Take My yoke upon you and learn from Me, for I am gentle
and lowly in heart, and you will find rest for your souls.
For My yoke is easy and My burden is light."
(Matthew 11:28-30 NKJV)

Day 13 of Encouragement

Flow like a mighty river
From the depths of the deepest well of my living waters
The waters of healing and refreshing
Bubbling up out of your innermost being
Let them rush over the grief, the wounds, the
hatred, the violence, the deception
Let them rush over the hurt, the pain and the disappointment
Let the waters cleanse with truth, holiness, purity and love
Let them spring forth with life, abundance, provision and protection
Flow, mighty river

"For waters shall burst forth in the wilderness, and streams in the desert."
(Isaiah 35:6 NKJV)

"The Lord will guide you continually, and satisfy your soul in
drought, and strengthen your bones; you shall be like a watered
garden, and like a spring of water, whose waters do not fail."
(Isaiah 58:11 NKJV)

"He who believes in Me, as the Scripture has said, out
of his heart will flow rivers of living water."
(John 7:38 NKJV)

Day 14 of Encouragement

Healing oil

Flowing over hearts, minds and bodies
Going deep into the crevices
Deep into the recesses of our minds
Healing oil to mend the broken heart
Healing oil to restore the disappointed spirit
Healing oil to strengthen the body
He is restoring
He is strengthening
He is healing
There is rest in His presence
There is peace in His presence
There is joy
He has come to redeem what was lost
He has come to bring restoration to what has been broken
His healing oil flows over and through us

"You kissed my heart with forgiveness, in spite of all I've done.
You've healed me inside and out from every disease."
(Psalms 103:3 TPT)

Day 15 of Encouragement

You will rise up in His mighty power
You will receive new strength
You will hear the voice of God and He will sustain you
You will see His handiwork in your body, in
your weakness and in your mind
He leads you beside the still waters and restores your soul
You are a threat to the enemy
He battles hard for you
But no weapon formed against you will prosper
because you still have your voice of triumph
You are not in fear but you are in power
You are not in stress but you are in peace
Your mind is set like a flint
You cannot be dismayed or swayed
You will not waver
You will stand firm
This is your victory
Rejoice

*"He giveth power to the faint; and to them that
have no might he increaseth strength."
(Isaiah 40:29 KJV)*

*"Fear thou not; for I am with thee: be not dismayed; for I am
thy God: I will strengthen thee; yea, I will help thee; yea, I
will uphold thee with the right hand of my righteousness."
(Isaiah 41:10 KJV)*

Day 16 of Encouragement

Communion

I let go of all dissension

I let go of all confusion

I let go of all disagreement

I let go of all negative words spoken to me or by me

I take on the mind of Christ

I bring every thought captive to the obedience of Christ

I embrace the identity of who God says I am

I receive His anointing

I receive His love

I am ready to pour out of my overflow of rivers of living water

I am ready to see the sick healed

I am ready to see the bound set free

Such as I have I give

"Stop imitating the ideals and opinions of the culture around you, but be inwardly transformed by the Holy Spirit through a total reformation of how you think. This will empower you to discern God's will as you live a beautiful life, satisfying and perfect in his eyes."
(Romans 12:2 TPT)

Day 17 of Encouragement

A new start always comes with a little apprehension and anxiety.
But it is the excitement of a new journey that brings
a new way of thinking, fresh ideas and fervor.
You are no longer concerned with what's always been,
but now you are ready to step into the new vision.
There is no longer a box to fit into but a new freedom
into a greater place of wonder and awe as you lead
others into the worship going on in the heavens.
You are stepping over a new threshold of bringing Heaven to earth.
You are opening another portal to see His glory come.
Stay in His presence.
Exemplify walking in the atmosphere you have made to
welcome Him at all times in all places with all people.
This is your opportunity to shine - not for yourself - not
in their presence - but for an audience of One.
Enjoy this journey ~
Don't try to figure it out
Simply follow His lead ~

*"With passion I pursue and cling to you. Because I feel your
grip on my life, I keep my soul close to your heart."
(Psalm 63:8 TPT)*

Day 18 of Encouragement

God is restoring your soul.
You have received wounds out of your own kindness and generosity.
God is removing this pain and the anguish.
He is pouring in the healing oil.
He is pulling out the arrows that have injured your heart.
You are precious to Him.
You are His heir.
You are His very own.
He says that the wounds you received were not yours but His.
Those who wounded you are not unhappy
with you but are not happy in Him.
They say with their words that they love Him but they have
not experienced the secret place of intimacy with Him.
They have their own wounds which they have
embraced instead of giving them to Him.
But you are being healed because your heart
cries out to Him in love and goodness.
He loves you with an everlasting love.

"Heal me, O LORD, and I shall be healed; Save me,
and I shall be saved, for You are my praise."
(Jeremiah 17:14 NKJV)

"Yes, I have loved you with an everlasting love"
(Jeremiah 31:3 NKJV)

Day 19 of Encouragement

Lean into Him
It seems as though you have received a sucker punch
But God is saying that your core is strong
Your strength comes from the Father alone
This is not a journey for you to walk alone
He will give you strategies
He will give you wisdom
He will be your provider
He will be your peace
He will be your joy
Release the anger
Release the hurt
Release the pain
It is painful because of the rejection and the betrayal but Jesus
has walked in these very moments and was victorious
He is walking with you now
He will not forsake you in the hour
Lean into Him
He is able to carry you, strengthen you and give you His wisdom
Walk with your head held high as the child of the Most High
You can be confident that He will complete what He started in you
He has promised to be your sustainer; let Him
Be at peace

*"He gives power to the weak, and to those who
have no might He increases strength.
Even the youths shall faint and be weary, and
the young men shall utterly fall,*

But those who wait on the LORD shall renew their strength;
they shall mount up with wings like eagles, they shall run
and not be weary, they shall walk and not faint."
(Isaiah 40:29-31)

Day 20 of Encouragement

The portals of Heaven are open over you
I am removing all of the dead things from your heart
The things that are no longer part of who you are
I'm removing the debris to make room for
more of my blessings and my gifts
I'm replacing these dead things with my
compassion, my peace, my love and my joy
You will flow in the fullness of my spirit as this has been your desire
You do not have to work to please me, for I
am pleased with you as my child
You do not have to impress me for you are my heart
Each time I touch you, another place has
been restored to my goodness
Each time I bless you, another breakthrough to
my anointing and favor is taking place
You will look back on these times and see how I transformed you
You will remember these days of transformation
and see the handiwork of my hands
This is a time of great preparation for I have so much more
for you, but you are not yet able to receive all of it
So take joy in the work I have started in you for I will complete it

*"I will give you a new heart and put a new spirit within you; I will
take the heart of stone out of your flesh and give you a heart of flesh.
I will put My Spirit within you and cause you to walk in My
statutes, and you will keep My judgments and do them."*
(Ezekiel 36:26-27)

Day 21 of Encouragement

The truth that the enemy has tried to hide
from you has been revealed to you.
You are no longer tied to the lies of the enemy.
You will rise to the truth of God.
You will no longer be in agreement with the deception,
accusations and intimidation of the enemy.

Place your hands over your ears and head

I silence the voice of the enemy and anoint my ears to
hear only the voice of God in regard to my identity.
I agree with the Word of the Lord.
It is not only faith over fear but truth over facts.
I am renewing my mind.
I am taking this step into freedom.
In Jesus' name ~

"And you shall know the truth, and the truth shall make you free."
(John 8:32)

Lightning Source UK Ltd.
Milton Keynes UK
UKHW041522120921
390324UK00013B/16